GREEN MATTE

Making Good Choices About
CONSERVATION

JANEY LEVY

rosen publishing's
**rosen
central**

New York

Published in 2010 by The Rosen Publishing Group, Inc.
29 East 21st Street, New York, NY 10010

Copyright © 2010 by The Rosen Publishing Group, Inc.

First Edition

Library of Congress Cataloging-in-Publication Data

Levy, Janey.
Making good choices about conservation / Janey Levy.
   p. cm.—(Green matters)
Includes bibliographical references and index.
ISBN-13: 978-1-4358-5314-0 (library binding)
ISBN-13: 978-1-4358-5610-3 (pbk)
ISBN-13: 978-1-4358-5611-0 (6 pack)
1. Conservation of natural resources—Juvenile literature. 2. Environmental protection—Juvenile literature. I. Title.
S940.L48 2010
333.72—dc22

2008046095

Manufactured in Malaysia

CONTENTS

INTRODUCTION

You've probably heard people talk about being "green." But do you know what it means? Being "green" means consciously choosing a lifestyle that's sustainable and environmentally friendly. It's important because this is the only world humans have. Humans can't simply move to the planet next door if they make this one uninhabitable.

Conservation is an important part of being green. It means taking care of natural resources—making careful decisions to avoid wasting or polluting them. Natural resources include air, freshwater, soil, forests, oceans, and biodiversity. Today, they're all endangered. A few examples convey the seriousness of the situation. The Nature Conservancy reports that, on average, each American puts 54,000 pounds (24,516 kilograms) of carbon dioxide (CO_2) into the air every year, causing significant air pollution. According to the Natural Resources Defense Council (NRDC), contaminated tap water sickens about seven million Americans annually. Modern industrialized farming practices, says the NRDC, have resulted in erosion that has carried away one-third of U.S. topsoil. According to Conservation International, 32 million acres (13 million hectares) of tropical forests—home to thousands of plant and animal species—are destroyed annually. Scientists Robert Diaz and Rutger Rosenberg reported in August 2008 that the world's oceans have more than four hundred dead zones—areas with too little oxygen to support life—covering about 94,500 square miles (245,000 square kilometers). According to the Millennium Ecosystem Assessment, 12 percent of bird species and 23 percent of mammal species face the threat of extinction.

Humans consume—and waste—far too much. Americans are some of the worst offenders. According to the editors of *E/The Environmental Magazine*, the United States has less than 5 percent of the world's people but consumes 33 percent of the world's materials. They also point out that the average U.S. consumer needs 30 acres (12.2 ha) to provide all the materials necessary to support his or her lifestyle, while the average Italian needs half that! Reducing consumption of natural resources and recycling and reusing as much as possible are essential conservation strategies.

Pollution created by humans also threatens the world. Much of that pollution results from the energy people use. The energy industry is the most polluting industry in the United States. The editors of *E/The Environmental Magazine* say the United States consumes nearly $1 million worth of energy every minute! So, reducing energy consumption is also an essential conservation strategy.

If you think the problems seem so big that nothing you do will make a difference, consider this: according to the NRDC, replacing just one regular light bulb with a compact fluorescent bulb (CFL) would keep half a ton (metric ton) of CO_2 out of the air over the bulb's lifetime. The U.S. Environmental Protection Agency (EPA) reports that if every home in the United States used just one CFL, it would reduce CO_2 emissions by an amount equal to the emissions of more than 800,000 cars! So you see, each person can make a difference. And together, people can make an even bigger difference.

Choosing Clean Air

The *Chandogya Upanishad*, an ancient Indian book of philosophy, tells of a quarrel among speech, eyes, ears, mind, and breath over which is most necessary for life. To settle the disagreement, they decide each function will abandon the body for a year, leaving the others to carry on without it. Afterward, they'll determine which proved to be most important. Speech leaves first, followed by eyes, ears, and mind. Through all this, life continues. As breath begins to depart, however, the other functions suddenly find themselves uprooted. They beseech breath to stay and acknowledge its primacy in sustaining life.

No one would dispute the story's truth. Humans can live for only a few minutes without breathing. And if breath is vital for life, so is clean air—not only for humans, but for animals and plants as well.

Today, the air is increasingly polluted. Industrial practices, transportation, and a wide range of human activities cause air pollution.

CAUSES OF AIR POLLUTION

Air pollution results when waste—in the form of gases or particulates (tiny particles of matter)—dirties the air. Some pollutants are toxic. Others produce damage through changes they cause in Earth's atmosphere.

Some pollution comes from natural sources. Volcanic eruptions, for example, may send particulates and toxic sulfur oxides (sulfur-oxygen compounds) into the atmosphere. Microorganisms in the digestive systems of cows and in rice fields produce a gas called methane. However, most experts believe that human activities produce most air pollution.

Exhaust fumes pour from cars at a traffic light in Denver, Colorado. Fifty times during one summer, the air was so polluted in Denver that it was declared unhealthy to breathe.

Industrial processes generate numerous pollutants, including ammonia, hydrocarbons (organic hydrogen-carbon compounds), sulfur oxides, and particulates containing lead and other harmful metals. Industry's transportation and electricity demands also contribute heavily to air pollution. Of course, the transportation and electricity demands of ordinary people contribute substantially, too.

Transportation is the leading cause of air pollution in most industrialized countries, including the United States and Canada. It produces carbon monoxide (CO), CO_2, hydrocarbons, and nitrogen oxides (nitrogen-oxygen compounds). These last two pollutants react in the presence of sunlight to form ozone, the main ingredient in photochemical smog.

Electricity production contributes significantly to air pollution. Most electricity in the United States and Canada is produced by burning oil, coal, or natural gas, putting nitrogen oxides, sulfur oxides, CO_2, and particulates into the air in the process.

Numerous ordinary activities also pollute the air. Burning trash releases harmful particulates and toxins, such as dioxins. Lighter fluid applied to charcoal in barbecue grills puts out harmful chemicals. Aerosol sprays send tiny droplets of the product into the air—and into your lungs. Filling your car with gasoline releases vapors that contribute to the formation of ozone. Cigarette smoke releases ten times more particulates than diesel car exhaust, according to a study conducted by Giovanni Invernizzi. And research by Congrong He, Lidia Morawska, and Len Taplin shows that some common laser printers produce as many particulates as cigarettes!

EFFECTS OF AIR POLLUTION

So, what are the consequences of all this air pollution? It harms living organisms, affects soil fertility, and even damages roads and buildings.

The coral shown here has been bleached, or damaged, by global warming resulting from air pollution. Some scientists fear global warming could destroy most coral reefs by 2100.

Air pollution worsens and sometimes causes asthma and other respiratory conditions. Particulates, ozone, sulfur dioxide (SO_2), and nitrogen oxides harm people's air passages and lungs. Carbon monoxide interferes with your blood's ability to deliver oxygen throughout your body. Some chemical compounds can cause cancer and birth defects.

Air pollutants hurt livestock and wild animals. They can damage or kill crops. They also harm forests.

Nitrogen oxides and SO_2 can produce acid rain, which pollutes rivers and lakes and harms the animals and plants living in them. Acid rain can also reduce soil fertility.

Air pollution damages human-made products. It harms plastics, rubber, and fabrics; dissolves concrete and stone; and causes metals to corrode more rapidly than usual.

Some air pollutants cause harm by altering Earth's atmosphere. Carbon dioxide, methane, and nitrous oxide (N_2O) are among the gases known as greenhouse gases. Just as a greenhouse's glass traps heat inside it, these gases trap the sun's heat on Earth. Naturally occurring greenhouse gases keep Earth warm enough to support life. However, human activities have significantly contributed to the greenhouse gas concentrations in the atmosphere and quite possibly could be causing Earth's overall temperature to rise. This effect is known as global warming or climate change. So far, it has produced severe droughts, terrible wildfires, deadly heat waves, stronger hurricanes, and floods, and it has damaged coral reefs, alpine meadows, and other habitats around the world. Scientists are also discovering that there is a rapid melting of glaciers, as well as Arctic and Antarctic ice. This melting threatens to raise ocean levels enough to cause severe coastal flooding and endanger polar bears, penguins, and other wildlife of these frozen regions. The situation is serious. Fortunately, there are actions each individual can take to help keep the air clean.

DID YOU KNOW?

According to the Nature Conservancy, the United States contributes about one-quarter of the world's greenhouse gas emissions each year—the equivalent of 54,000 pounds (24,500 kg) of CO_2 per person. How does the United States manage to generate such high emission levels? Consider these figures. On average, each person in the United States annually produces the equivalent of the following:

- 17,000 pounds (7,700 kg) of CO_2 by using 1,100 kilowatt-hours of electricity each month
- 1,000 pounds (454 kg) of CO_2 by creating 4.5 pounds (2 kg) of trash daily
- 8,900 pounds (4,040 kg) of CO_2 by driving 160 miles (260 km) per week

STEPS YOU AND YOUR FAMILY CAN TAKE TO REDUCE AIR POLLUTION

It requires conscious decisions and effort, but each person can help reduce air pollution by reducing his or her carbon footprint. Since transportation is the leading cause of air pollution, that's a good place to start. The Nature Conservancy reports that personal cars and trucks produce 20 percent of U.S. carbon emissions. So, walk or ride your bicycle whenever you can. If you live in a place that has good public transportation, use it.

Riding a bicycle instead of using a car isn't an option only for young people. Many adults, like the man shown here, choose to use bicycles to get to work.

Sometimes, using a car is necessary, so drivers should develop driving habits that save fuel. Combine errands instead of making lots of short trips. Avoid "jackrabbit" starts and excessive braking, which burn extra fuel. Drive the speed limit. Gasoline mileage decreases at speeds more than 55 miles (88 km) per hour. Make sure your tires are properly inflated because low tire pressure reduces gasoline mileage. Refuel after dusk. That reduces the amount of ozone-causing fumes that escape. Be careful not to spill gasoline because the spilled fuel releases fumes. If your family plans to buy a new car, purchase the most fuel-efficient one that your family can afford.

There are still other ways to reduce gasoline usage. For example, buy local food and goods whenever possible. Because they haven't been transported great distances, they haven't required a lot of gasoline to get to you. Gasoline-powered lawn mowers contribute to air pollution. According to a report by Anders Christensen, Roger Westerholm, and Jacob Almén, running a gasoline-powered lawn mower for one hour creates about the same amount of air pollution as a 100-mile (161-km) car ride! So, if your family has a gasoline-powered lawn mower, consider getting an old-fashioned reel mower.

Because generating electricity produces substantial amounts of air pollution, reduce your electricity usage. Climb the stairs instead of using the elevator or escalator. Use compact fluorescent lightbulbs

Old-fashioned reel, or push, mowers are much more environmentally friendly than gasoline or electric mowers. They can even help improve the user's physical fitness because they provide better exercise.

(CFLs) and dispose of them properly when they're exhausted (check your local recycling programs). Turn off lights and unplug electronics and appliances when they're not in use. Even when they're turned off, they still use some electricity when they're plugged in. Use appliances efficiently. That is, wash full loads of clothes and run the dishwasher only when it's full. Set the thermostat lower in the winter and higher in the summer. Turn the temperature on your water heater down to 120°F (50°C) instead of 140°F (60°C). If your family is planning on buying new appliances, choose energy-efficient models. Weatherize your home to reduce the amount of heat it loses in winter or lets in during summer. In some places, electricity providers allow customers to choose

Many communities have recycling programs. Residents fill specially marked containers with recyclable items and place them by the curb for collection. If your community has a program, be sure to participate in it!

electricity generated by renewable, nonpolluting sources. Do that if you have the option. And always reduce, recycle, and reuse. Taking those steps greatly reduces the amount of electricity used to produce goods and the amount of fuel needed to transport them.

There are other measures you can take, too. Avoid aerosols and other products that pollute the air. Don't smoke. Don't burn trash. Write to government leaders to urge them to create laws that protect clean air. And encourage everyone you know to help keep the air clean!

CHAPTER ②

Keeping Rivers and Lakes Clean

Seen from space, Earth appears mostly blue. That's because water covers more than 70 percent of Earth's surface.

Water is essential for life. Inside living organisms, it carries nutrients to every cell and carries waste products away. Every living organism on Earth consists mostly of water. Your body is about two-thirds water. An elephant is about 70 percent water. A tomato is about 90 percent water!

People—plus land plants and animals and those living in rivers and lakes—need freshwater to exist. Freshwater is more vital for your survival than food. You can live for weeks without food but only about a week without water. In spite of freshwater's importance, people endanger it through many of their actions.

DANGERS TO FRESHWATER

Toxic industrial wastes. Untreated sewage. Chemical fertilizers and pesticides from farms. Perhaps you picture those scenes when you think about water pollution.

The bubbles all along the base of this waterfall provide a clear visual indication that phosphates from detergents or fertilizers have polluted the water.

But other dangers lurk in the products people use and the activities they perform every day.

Air pollution—which, as you learned in chapter 1, can result from numerous common activities—can cause acid rain. Acid rain harms rivers and lakes, killing fish and other wildlife.

Many common household and personal-care products contain toxic ingredients. These toxins get washed through drains, sinks, and toilets into rivers and lakes. They harm fish and wildlife and increase not only the cost of creating clean water but also the amount of pollution-generating energy needed to clean the water.

Phosphates in detergents and in lawn and garden fertilizers cause water pollution. They greatly increase the growth of algae. When the algae die, their decay uses up the water's oxygen, killing other life in the water.

A chemical used to make freshwater safe to drink also causes damage. U.S. and Canadian laws require the addition of chlorine to kill harmful bacteria. Unfortunately, chlorine also kills helpful bacteria and is highly toxic to fish. In people, it can cause allergic reactions and has been linked to heart disease and cancer.

People also waste water and thus must use more energy to produce more clean water and deliver it to homes, schools, and businesses. Increased energy usage leads to increased pollution that harms water. Fortunately, you have the power to make a difference.

STEPS YOU AND YOUR FAMILY CAN TAKE TO REDUCE WATER POLLUTION

Each person can help reduce water pollution. For starters, don't pour hazardous household products down the sink drain or flush them down the toilet. Instead, dispose of them through your town's hazardous waste program. If your community doesn't have a program, ask for one. In addition, never flush unwanted medicines down the toilet or wash them down the drain. Take them to a pharmacy for safe disposal (many states and drugstores do have disposal programs), or take them

At this drop-off center in Seattle, Washington, volunteers wearing gloves, aprons, and gas masks dispose of hazardous household products.

out of their containers and throw them in the trash. Many medicines are unable to be broken down into simpler substances by bacteria (that is, they are not biodegradable). They could pass through treatment plants and still be in recycled water that communities use.

Avoid detergents and other polluting household cleaners. Instead, use baking soda, vinegar, natural citrus products, and cornstarch as cleaning agents. Baking soda and citrus products clean sinks, tubs, toilets, and showers, and they brighten laundry. Vinegar cuts grease and removes mildew. Cornstarch can be used to clean windows and shampoo carpets and rugs.

Choose personal-care products that don't contain detergents or toxic ingredients. Look for organic or natural products with plant-based

Seventh Generation produces environmentally friendly household products. The company's paper products, such as the toilet paper shown here, are made from recycled paper and are bleached without chlorine.

ingredients. Not only will they help protect Earth's water, but they'll also be better for your health.

Buy clothing made from organic cotton or hemp. These fibers come from plants grown sustainably, without chemical fertilizers and pesticides. Some companies also offer clothing colored with environmentally friendly earth and plant dyes.

Buy paper products that haven't been bleached with chlorine. Look for products labeled TCF (totally chlorine-free) or PCF (processed chlorine-free).

Use natural fertilizers, such as compost or manure, on lawns and gardens. You may be able to buy these fertilizers locally. You can also

GRAY WATER

Some people use gray water to reduce their freshwater usage. Gray water is wastewater from showers, baths, and laundry. Instead of letting it go down the drain, some people use it for composting and to water lawns and gardens.

Given that gray water contains soap, detergent, germs, and perhaps other matter, some precautions are required. Filter it to remove hair, lint, and other solids. Don't use it on plants that will be eaten. Use flood or drip watering for lawns and gardens, rather than sprinklers. Don't let gray water run off your property.

Be aware that some areas prohibit or limit the use of gray water. So, before doing anything, make sure that using gray water is legal where you live.

do your own composting. There are composting canisters you can buy that store the material, speed up decomposition, and have activated carbon filters that reduce or eliminate odors.

Reduce, recycle, and reuse in all areas of your life. Producing and transporting goods and food uses energy and creates pollution that often winds up in lakes and rivers. The more people consume, the more pollution they create.

EASY WAYS TO REDUCE WATER WASTE

Some simple changes in your behavior can save water. Start in the kitchen. Instead of wasting tap water waiting for it to get cold enough to drink, keep drinking water in the refrigerator. Instead of letting water run down the drain while waiting for it to get hot, collect that water in a container and use it to water plants. If you wash dishes by hand, don't leave the water running the whole time. If you have a dishwasher, don't rinse dirty dishes before loading them; just scrape them. Run the dishwasher only when it's full.

Avoid waste in the bathroom, too. Don't leave the water running while you brush your teeth or shave. Take shorter showers. According to Environment Canada, a ten-minute shower uses about 53 gallons (200 liters) of water. If you take a five-minute shower instead, you can save more than 185 gallons (700 l) of water every week.

Fix leaks and drips. According to the Natural Resources Defense Council, a dripping faucet can waste 20 gallons (76 l) of water each day. A leaking toilet can waste 200 gallons (757 l)!

If you have a garden, grow only plants native to your area. They're adapted to thrive there without a lot of extra water. Sprinklers lose water to evaporation. Use a soaker hose instead. Collect rain in a barrel for watering your plants. A fine mesh screen can prevent mosquitoes from breeding in the water. However, make sure your community allows standing water. Some prohibit it completely because there's always a risk that disease-bearing mosquitoes may breed.

Your family may want to consider replacing older equipment with more energy-efficient models. Front-loading washing machines use only about one-third to one-fourth the amount of water that a top-loading washer does. However, they're also very expensive to buy and thus not a good option for everyone. If a front-loading washing machine isn't right for your family, consider a new energy-efficient top-loader. They can reduce water usage by up to one-half.

Older toilets use 3.5 gallons (13.3 l) per flush. Newer ones use 1.6 gallons (6 l) or less. Some toilets even have one flush button for solid waste and a second for liquid waste. They use 1.6 gallons to flush solid waste and only 0.8 gallon (3 l) to flush liquid waste! If replacing an older toilet isn't possible, fill a 1-gallon (4 l) plastic bottle

The bright yellow Energy Guide sticker that is placed on appliances indicates how energy efficient a particular model is compared to the most- and least-efficient models of the appliance.

with water and put it in the toilet tank. By taking up space, it reduces the amount of water in the tank and thus the amount used per flush.

Put low-flow aerators on sink faucets and showerheads. They mix air with the water and reduce the amount of water used by about half.

These are only some of the ways to reduce your water usage. You can probably think of others. As the numbers show, even just a few changes can make a big difference. Spread the word—talk with your family and friends to let them know how easy it is to conserve water!

MYTH: People can protect themselves from high levels of particulate air pollution outside by simply staying indoors.

FACT: When particulate levels are high outdoors, they're high indoors, too. The only way to avoid exposure to dangerous levels of particulates is to keep particulate levels low.

MYTH: Conserving water will force people to make major changes in their lifestyles.

FACT: Everyone can conserve a lot of water through simple changes in behavior that reduce waste.

MYTH: Logging in national forests will protect them by preventing disastrous forest fires and diseases.

FACT: Fire is a natural part of a healthy forest ecosystem, so trying to completely suppress fires isn't desirable. However, commercial logging changes forest ecosystems in ways that result in more severe fires and more tree deaths from disease.

CHAPTER ③

Making Choices for Safe, Healthy Soil

Soil. It's almost everywhere. Many people probably take it for granted. Yet, it's one of the most important natural resources. All life on Earth depends on soil. Plants grow in soil and get essential nutrients from it. Animals—including humans—get the nutrients they need to survive from plants or from animals that eat plants.

Soil consists of minerals combined with organic matter. The minerals come from the weathering, or wearing away, of rocks. The organic matter, called humus, comes from decomposing, or rotting, plant and animal remains. Healthy, fertile soil contains not only minerals and humus but also bacteria, which break down the humus into the nutrients plants need.

Soil is constantly being formed, so you might think there is no need to worry about it. However, the process of soil formation is slow. It has taken thousands of years to form the

Many home gardeners create their own nutrient-rich compost for their soil. They combine dead plant matter, grass clippings, vegetable and fruit scraps, coffee grounds, and water, and allow the mix to decay.

thin layer of fertile soil that covers the land. Yet, human activities can destroy that essential layer of fertile soil in just a few years.

HARMFUL HUMAN PRACTICES

A leading problem in soil conservation is erosion. Generally, erosion happens gradually. Human practices have greatly increased the rate of soil erosion, though, threatening this precious resource.

Much erosion results from the removal of vegetation to clear land for construction. The plants that were removed protected the soil from the potentially damaging effects of wind and rain. Their roots held the

Some farming practices contribute to soil erosion. As this farmer tills his field on a windy day, the wind picks up loose particles of soil and blows them away.

soil in place. In addition, the plants absorbed some of the rainwater, so there was less to run off the land and carry soil away. Similar problems occur in places where the timber industry practices clear-cutting, which is the removal of all trees in an area.

Overgrazing also contributes to erosion. If ranchers allow herds to graze too long in an area, it reduces the amount of organic matter in the soil. As a result, the soil erodes easily.

Clearing land for farmland plays a role in erosion, too. You may think that is odd. After all, farmers grow crops on their land. Don't the crops help hold the soil in place in the same way wild plants do? Not necessarily. Unlike wild plants, crops don't grow in the fields year-round.

HOW DO YOU KNOW IF IT'S REALLY ORGANIC?

Buying organic food is a good way to support sustainable farming practices. For food to be considered organic, it must be produced without chemical fertilizers and pesticides and be processed with only natural additives (such as those manufactured from soybeans, corn, or beets). But how do you know if a food is organic? For fresh fruits and vegetables, look at the Price Look-Up (PLU) code, which is the code of numerals printed on the tiny sticker that is attached to the item. If it begins with 9, the fruit or vegetable is organic. For other food items—such as flour, pasta sauce, fruit juice, and prepared foods—read the label carefully. If it has the USDA (United States Department of Agriculture) organic seal, it's made with at least 95 percent organic ingredients. Foods that have at least 70 percent organic ingredients can use the claim "Made with Organic Ingredients."

In addition, some farming practices increase erosion. According to the NRDC, one-third of the topsoil in the United States has been lost as a result of modern industrialized farming practices. One culprit is tilling, or plowing. Before planting, the land must be prepared through tilling. Conventional tillage removes most of the crop residue, the plant matter left from the previous harvest. Since that residue helps prevent erosion, removing most of it increases erosion. To prevent the problem, some farmers practice conservation tillage, which leaves at least 30 percent of the residue on the field. The timing of tillage is also a factor. It's best to leave the residue on fields through winter to prevent erosion from rain and melting snow in the spring. However, a wet spring can force a farmer to delay tilling and planting, resulting in a smaller crop yield. Therefore, some farmers till in the fall, after the harvest, leaving fields exposed to erosion in the spring.

The practice of planting the same crop in a field year after year can reduce soil fertility. Corn, wheat, and some other grain crops drain nitrogen, an essential nutrient, from the soil. Farmers can avoid the problem by practicing crop rotation, alternating the nitrogen-draining crop with such crops as alfalfa or soybeans, which add nitrogen to the soil.

Chemical pesticides and fertilizers—used by home gardeners as well as farmers—also harm the soil. The chemicals can reduce the ability of the soil's bacteria to break down the humus. The soil may become harder as a result, making it less able to absorb water and thus easier to erode. The chemicals cause other problems, too. They can be washed into rivers and lakes, polluting the waters, and have been linked to cancer and other health problems in humans.

STEPS YOU AND YOUR FAMILY CAN TAKE TO PROTECT THE SOIL

There are many measures that you and your family can take to help protect the soil. Buy organic food. When you can, purchase local organic food. Buying organic helps the local economy and reduces air pollution because the food didn't have to be transported a great distance to reach you. Buying local also gives you a chance to find out what kind of tillage a farmer practices. Purchasing food from local farmers who practice conservation tillage is a good way to protect the soil, even if their produce doesn't qualify as organic.

Don't limit your organic buying to foods. Buy clothing made from organic cotton and hemp. Organic cotton is grown without the use of damaging chemical pesticides and fertilizers, whereas conventionally grown cotton depends heavily on both. Hemp produces vastly more

Chemical pesticides are sometimes sprayed over farm fields by airplanes. The wind may carry some of the pesticides away, spreading the harm they may create far beyond the farm field.

fiber than cotton, without the use of pesticides, and it also adds nitrogen to the soil. Buy organic personal-care products, too. In terms of household products, you may not be able to buy organic products, but you can choose products that don't contribute to soil pollution or erosion. For example, buy paper products with a high recycled paper content to reduce the number of trees destroyed. Avoid chemical pesticides.

If you have a garden at home, make it organic, and do your own composting to fertilize it. Grow plants native to your area. They're adapted to grow in the existing soil conditions, without requiring the addition of chemicals that could be harmful. Make sure you and your family do garden and yard planting in a way that helps prevent erosion. For example, you can plant a rain garden to capture runoff water and keep it from washing soil away. If you have a lawn, leave grass clippings on the lawn after mowing to enrich the soil. Walk around your yard in aerator sandals. The spikes on the bottom can help loosen the soil and are an effective way to kill some lawn pests.

If your family uses oil heat and stores fuel oil in an underground tank, there are precautions you must take to protect the environment. The tank could rust, resulting in leaks and contamination of the soil with fuel oil. If your family notices that you seem to be using more fuel, have the tank tested for leaks. In fact, it should be tested regularly so that small problems can be detected before they become large ones. Know the local, county, and state regulations that apply to fuel oil storage tanks, and make sure your family's tank meets them. If you need to get a new tank, get one that's double walled and has a monitor.

Although you may be getting tired of reading this advice—reduce, recycle, and reuse! Those are some of the most effective steps you can take for all aspects of conservation. Finally, write to your government leaders about the problems caused by chemical fertilizers and pesticides, and urge them to make laws that encourage and support more environmentally friendly soil practices.

CHAPTER ④

Forest-Friendly Living

Have you ever visited a forest? Forests are beautiful, amazing places, filled not only with trees but also with many other types of plants and animals. They are the most richly diverse ecosystems on land, with their plant and animal species varying according to location. Unfortunately, forests are severely endangered. People have been cutting down forests for farmland and cities ever since agriculture began about eleven thousand years ago. According to the NRDC, forests once covered almost 50 percent of Earth's land, or about 18 billion acres (7 billion ha). According to the Worldwatch Institute, people have destroyed about 7.5 billion acres (3 billion ha) of that original forest cover. And deforestation continues today at an alarming rate. In 2008, Oakley Brooks reports in *Nature Conservancy* that an area roughly the size of New York State—about 32 million acres (13 million ha)— is destroyed annually. This loss matters because forests are important for many reasons.

The red area in this photograph is deforested land in the Amazon rain forest. Between August 2003 and August 2004, more than 10,000 square miles (26,000 sq km) were destroyed.

EARTH'S VALUABLE FORESTS AND THE THREATS THEY FACE

The world's forests have many kinds of value. One is economic value. Wood from forests is used in building; for making furniture, tool handles, and thousands of other products; and as fuel for heating and cooking. It's also used to make paper and processed wood products like cellophane, some plastics, and even fibers like rayon, which is used in clothing. Besides wood, forests provide latex (which is used to make rubber), fruits, nuts, fats, oils, gums, waxes, and resins.

This photograph shows a recently discovered pygmy possum in the Indonesian rain forest. The tiny possum and millions more creatures may disappear forever if their forest homes are destroyed.

Forests also have medical value. Rain forests, for example, have yielded thousands of medicines to fight diseases like malaria, glaucoma (an eye disease), and cancer. A muscle relaxant sometimes used in heart surgery also comes from a rain forest plant. All of these medicines come from the 1 percent of rain forest plants tested by scientists. The remaining 99 percent may hold untold thousands more!

Forests have environmental value as well. They absorb large amounts of rainwater, preventing the rapid runoff that can result in erosion and flooding, and keeping rivers clean by preventing soil and pollutants from getting washed into them. Forests help renew the atmosphere. During photosynthesis, they give off oxygen, which people and all other animals need to breathe. They also remove CO_2, one of the greenhouse gases, from the air.

Forests have cultural value. Many societies have legends, myths, or folk tales that feature forests. In some places, such as South America and New Guinea, people have lived in forests for centuries and have developed cultures centered on the forest. Without the forests, these cultures break down.

Forests have recreational value. Every year, millions of people enjoy visiting forests and hiking, camping, or simply appreciating their beauty.

Forests also provide crucial habitat for thousands of wildlife species, many of which can live nowhere else. Tropical rain forests, for example, are home to more than half the plant and animal species on Earth, although they cover only about 6 percent of the planet. Andrew Downie reports that Brazil's Atlantic Forest, although greatly reduced from the millions of acres it once covered, is home to one thousand bird species and twenty-six primate species. Two hundred of the bird species and twenty-one of the primate species are found nowhere else.

Tropical rain forests play an important role in regulating Earth's climate. By absorbing the sun's light and heat, they help regulate temperatures not only in their immediate region but also around the world.

THE FOREST STEWARDSHIP COUNCIL

The Forest Stewardship Council (FSC) is a nonprofit, nongovernmental organization founded by loggers, foresters, environmentalists, and sociologists in 1993. Its goal is to promote the responsible, sustainable management of forests around the world. It sets standards that take into account the protection of forest watersheds, soil, and native species; restrictions on the use of chemicals; and fair labor policies. It certifies companies whose practices meet its standards. Those companies are then entitled to put the FSC label on their products. So, when your family needs to buy wood products, including paper, the FSC label can help you choose sustainably produced goods.

By taking in and holding on to CO_2, they help prevent the buildup of this greenhouse gas in the air. When tropical rain forests are destroyed, all that CO_2 they've been holding—sometimes for centuries—is released back into the atmosphere. Scientists estimate that deforestation currently contributes about 17 percent of the world's CO_2 emissions. That's more than the total emissions of all the cars, trucks, buses, trains, and planes in the world! So, threats to forests threaten Earth's environment as a whole.

Today, deforestation resulting from commercial logging and clearing land for agriculture endangers forests. So does air pollution, which leads to acid rain, as well as soil and water pollution. Fortunately, you and your family can make choices that will help protect Earth's forests.

FOREST-FRIENDLY CHOICES

People buy wood and wood products for many reasons. Perhaps they need a new piece of furniture. Perhaps they're building a deck on their house or maybe even a whole new house. They can face a dizzying array of choices while shopping, and it can be hard to determine which choice is the most environmentally friendly. But there are actions that each person can take to help ensure that the wood or wood product being purchased has been sustainably harvested.

Look for the logo of the Forest Stewardship Council (FSC). It certifies that the wood comes from a responsibly and sustainably managed forest. If you can't find wood or wood products certified by the FSC, ask where the wood comes from. Woods from some places—especially hardwoods—are harvested in unsustainable ways. Hardwoods, often sought after by consumers, pose particular problems because they grow much more slowly than softwoods. Buying woods harvested in unsustainable ways may also contribute to cruel and unacceptable labor practices, since such wood may have been harvested using forced labor. Among the woods associated with poor practices are big-leaf mahogany, African mahogany, Spanish cedar, Caribbean pine, rosewood, and teak. So, avoid lumber and furniture made from those woods.

You can also help protect forests by buying products made with wood substitutes, such as bamboo. Or, consider salvaged or recycled wood. You may not think of wood as something that can be recycled, but it can be, and it's one way to conserve forests. Many people like the look of wood reclaimed from old barns, for example. You and your family may also be able to get doors and window frames from salvage companies.

Many trees are logged to make paper and paper products. So, you can help protect forests by choosing paper products with recycled paper content. The higher the recycled content, the greater the reduction in new trees harvested. This applies to notebooks, printer paper, napkins, toilet paper, paper towels, and any other paper products you use. You should also look for ways to reduce the amount of paper you use. Do you really need to print that e-mail or that funny story you found online? How about using cloth napkins instead of paper napkins, or old cloths for cleaning, rather than paper towels? Reuse paper, too. Instead of throwing out paper with printing or writing on only one side, save it to use as scrap paper.

There are other steps that you can take to protect forests as well. If you're going camping and will need firewood, buy wood where you'll be camping, rather than taking wood from home. Wood brought into

This furniture display is meant to remind consumers that their choices have environmental consequences and that it is important to consider those consequences when selecting furniture. Choose wood from certified sustainable forests, vegetable-based stains, and eco-friendly fabric, if possible.

an area from outside may carry invasive insects or diseases that can destroy trees. After hiking in a forest, clean your shoes or boots to avoid the risk of spreading diseases from that forest to the next place you hike. Join campaigns to plant trees to restore damaged forests. Avoid contributing to air, water, and soil pollution, which harm forests. Write to government leaders to urge them to pass laws protecting forests. And educate your family and friends about the importance of forests, dangers they face, and ways to protect them. You can also help contribute to essential climate benefits, particularly in urban areas, by planting trees. Not only do trees absorb carbon from the atmosphere while releasing oxygen back into the air, but they also help cool the air by providing shade in hot weather. Shade can offer protection from harmful ultraviolet rays (especially the UVB type) that have been associated with some human skin cancers.

CHAPTER 5

Showing Concern for Oceans

Do you remember reading in chapter 2 that Earth appears mostly blue from space because water covers more than 70 percent of its surface? Well, most of that water is ocean. The oceans contain about 97 percent of all the water on Earth. Most scientists believe life on Earth began in the oceans about 3.5 billion years ago.

You may be thinking, fine, oceans cover most of Earth and hold most of Earth's water. But ocean water is salt water. People—and land animals in general—can't drink it. Crops and other land plants can't grow with it. And it's not as if we're running out of ocean water; there's plenty. So, why worry about the oceans? Oceans provide many benefits both for people and for the planet as a whole. Without the oceans, there would be no life on Earth.

THE IMPORTANCE OF OCEANS

Hundreds of thousands of plant and animal species live in the world's oceans. Many

This underwater turbine uses tidal power to generate electricity. A Scottish power company recently announced plans to create an underwater energy "farm" with up to sixty turbines.

others—penguins and sea otters are just two examples—depend on oceans for food. People depend on oceans for food, too. People harvest millions of tons of fish and shellfish every year. In some places, seafood is people's main source of protein. Many people eat ocean plants such as kelp, too.

Besides food, people obtain medicines from the oceans. Chemicals from marine organisms help fight cancer and viruses and help treat severe pain. Scientists believe they may discover many more medicines as they learn about the wealth of life in the oceans.

Ocean sediments gathered from the sea floor are used in construction and to restore damaged beaches. They also contain useful minerals like magnesium, which is used in the manufacture of a range of products.

The oceans are sources of energy. Rich deposits of oil and gas lie beneath the ocean floor. You've probably seen pictures of the offshore wells employed to draw out these resources. But did you know that the oceans themselves can provide energy? In some places, the rise and fall of tides is used to produce electricity.

Believe it or not, some coastal communities also get drinking water from the ocean. The salt is removed in a process called desalination, making the water fit for humans to drink, cook with, and use to water their crops. The first tidal power plant opened in France in 1966. Even ocean waves may one day be used to create electricity!

In addition to these benefits, there's another very important one—the oceans play a major role in regulating Earth's climate. Water changes temperature much more slowly than the air. In summer, the oceans take in and store heat. In winter, they slowly release it. Ocean currents carry heat from tropical waters toward the poles. This keeps the tropics from getting too hot and warms the regions near the poles. Oceans also absorb and store CO_2, helping prevent the buildup of this greenhouse gas in the atmosphere. In spite of the enormous importance of the oceans, thoughtless human activities have endangered them.

These men are checking the quality of frozen tuna before selling it. Tuna's enormous popularity among consumers around the globe has led to overfishing that threatens the world's tuna fisheries.

DANGERS TO OCEANS

Overfishing—capturing fish faster than they can reproduce—poses a major threat to the world's oceans. Modern technology has enabled commercial fishing operations to vastly increase their catch. As a result, fisheries around the world have collapsed. And the consequences extend beyond individual species. Overfishing changes entire marine ecosystems and affects local economies, leaving fishermen with no way to earn a living.

Commercial fishing practices also result in enormous amounts of bycatch—unwanted or unintentional catch. Millions of tons of fish,

43

FISH FARMING: THE GOOD AND THE BAD

Many people consider seafood an important part of a healthy diet. Fish farming, or aquaculture, supplies much of that seafood, and its ecological effect may be good or bad. Oysters, clams, and mussels are usually farmed in environmentally friendly ways. Because they feed by filtering tiny ocean organisms called plankton out of the water, they may actually help clean the water where they're raised. However, all aquaculture isn't environmentally friendly. Fish that feed on other fish, for example, are fed with wild fish, increasing rather than reducing the demand on wild fisheries. Farming plant-eating fish like tilapia avoids those problems. Farming fish in net pens in coastal waters pollutes the waters with an enormous amount of waste. Diseases can spread to wild fish in the area, and drugs used to treat the diseases may leak into the surrounding waters. Farming fish inland, where the wastes can be removed, helps protect oceans.

as well as sea turtles, marine mammals like dolphins, and even sea-birds, die as bycatch every year.

Fish practices that involve dragging nets across the ocean floor cause immense damage to fragile habitats. It can take centuries for those habitats to recover.

Nutrients from fertilizers and livestock manure often make their way from fields to rivers and then to oceans, where they have the same harmful effects they do in freshwater. They can cause algae overgrowths that create enormous dead zones by using up oxygen, damage fragile coral reefs, or—because of toxins—kill fish and marine mammals and sicken people.

Heavy coastal development also damages oceans. Runoff from storms carries pollutants like motor oil, trash, fertilizers, and pesticides. Trash left on beaches often winds up in the ocean.

Numerous other human activities threaten oceans. Military sonar testing causes whales and other marine mammals to strand themselves on beaches. Noise and water pollution from ships and offshore drilling disrupts the migration routes, feeding, and mating of marine animals. Global warming and ocean acidification from too much CO_2 in the water damage coral reefs, harming the entire reef ecosystem. Ocean acidification also interferes with shellfish growth.

What can you do about these problems? There are several steps you and your family can take to protect the world's oceans.

WAYS TO PROTECT THE OCEANS

Fighting pollution is an important part of ocean conservation, and there are numerous ways to do it. Many of the steps outlined earlier for combating freshwater and air pollution are also important for battling ocean pollution. That's because pollution in rivers and the air often makes its way into oceans. For example, when levels of the greenhouse gas CO_2 are high, the excess CO_2 dissolves into water on the ocean's surface, causing ocean acidification. So, work to reduce your carbon footprint. Cut back on how much electricity you use. Walk, ride your bicycle, or use public transportation instead of driving. Buy local, organic food. Less CO_2 goes into the air because the food hasn't been transported as far. Since it's been grown without chemical fertilizers or pesticides, it's not adding those pollutants to Earth's waters. Avoid using chemical fertilizers or pesticides on home lawns and gardens as well. Planting native species helps,

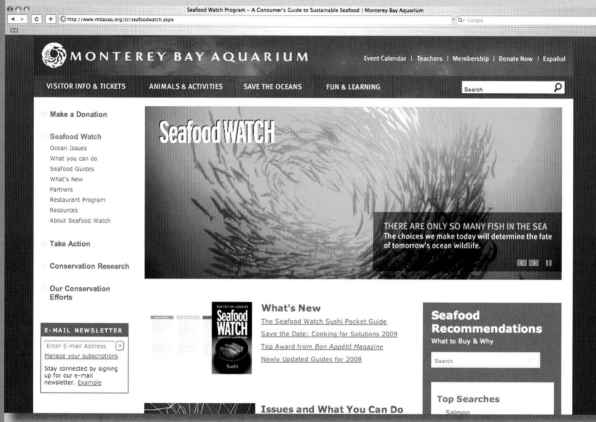

Go to Monterey Bay Aquarium's Web site (http://www.mbayaq.org/cr/SeafoodWatch.asp) for information on how to make wise seafood choices. Check out the rest of the Web site for more information about ocean conservation.

since they're adapted to grow in local conditions. Choose green household cleaners. Dispose of household hazardous wastes properly; don't pour them down the drain or flush them down the toilet. Reduce your use of plastic items. These often wind up in oceans, where wildlife may become entangled in them or be harmed by mistaking them for food. If you visit a beach, don't leave trash behind. Dispose of it properly.

Ocean conservation involves other steps as well. Whether you're eating at home or dining out, choose seafood that's been caught or raised in a sustainable, environmentally friendly way. The Monterey Bay Aquarium offers a seafood guide that you can print from its Web site and carry with you to help you make informed choices. Don't buy jewelry or other items made from real coral. Write to government leaders about the importance of protecting coastal wetlands, which help filter pollutants from runoff and keep it from entering ocean waters. Also, encourage government leaders to create protected underwater parks, just as protected national parks have been created on land. And talk with friends and family about the importance of ocean conservation.

CHAPTER 6

Making Decisions That Benefit Biodiversity

Have you ever heard of the term "biodiversity"? Do you know what it means? It's short for "biological diversity," and it refers to the variety of species on Earth, the genes they contain, and the ecosystems they form. Most often, people mean "species diversity" when they talk about biodiversity. But it's not really possible to separate the kinds of biodiversity. They're interconnected, and changes in one type of biodiversity will affect all forms.

Maintaining biodiversity is a major concern of conservationists and environmentalists. Some people wonder, however, if it's really that important. Does it matter if there are fewer frog or butterfly species? Such questions are really asking whether or not it matters to humans if there are fewer species. The answer is yes. As the first paragraph points out, everything is interconnected. Humans are part of this web, although they often mistakenly think of themselves as outside of it.

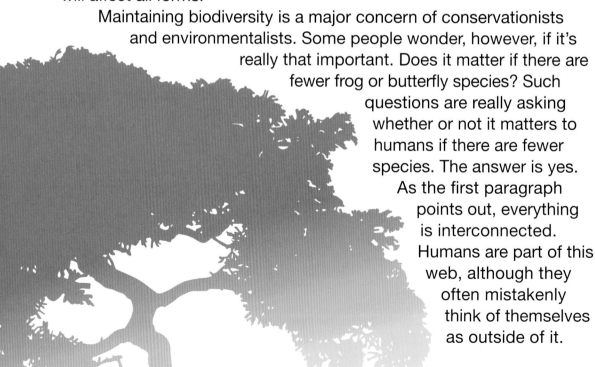

And changes in one part of it affect the whole. That idea may seem pretty abstract, but scientists identify several concrete reasons why biodiversity is important.

BENEFITS OF BIODIVERSITY AND DANGERS IT FACES

Although people often don't recognize it, humans depend on biodiversity every day. It provides what scientists call "ecosystem services." That term describes many practical benefits people receive from Earth's diverse ecosystems. They provide clean air and water, create and maintain fertile soil, pollinate crops, break down waste, and recycle

This tiny, poisonous red frog was photographed at Costa Rica's National Biodiversity Institute. The institute's mission is to gather knowledge on the country's biodiversity and promote sustainable use of it.

nutrients. To provide these services, though, the ecosystems must remain healthy, and since every organism in an ecosystem has a role to play, all organisms are important.

Biodiversity also furnishes humans with food and medicines. Scientists believe that many plants and animals we know little about may one day provide nutritious food and medicines to fight terrible diseases.

Biodiversity has economic benefits as well. According to the Biodiversity Project, activities like food production, hunting, and nature tourism—which all rely on biodiversity—contribute as much as $33 trillion to the global economy. The benefit to the U.S. economy alone is about $300 billion annually. The other side of the coin is that the loss of biodiversity and healthy ecosystems costs money. People must pay to clean their air and water. Less food is produced.

Finally, biodiversity provides natural beauty. If you've ever visited a state or national park, or even simply walked through an unspoiled natural area near your home, you've had a chance to enjoy the beauty of nature. For all these reasons, biodiversity is important. It's also in danger.

Many current human actions threaten biodiversity. As the human population grows, it requires increasing amounts of food. Humans consume more and more of the planet's resources. Overhunting and overfishing push species to the edge of extinction. Humans create pollution that harms resources, and they build cities and clear land without adequate consideration of the environmental impact. They destroy habitats. They introduce invasive species that upset the balance of ecosystems. They fuel global warming, which threatens to throw all of Earth's ecosystems out of balance. It's important for people to take action to protect Earth's biodiversity.

WAYS TO PROTECT BIODIVERSITY

The list of things you can do to protect biodiversity is almost endless. That's because all the steps you take to conserve air, water, soil,

UNINTENDED CONSEQUENCES

Writing for the Web site Global Issues, Anup Shah recounts a story told in a *National Geographic Wild* television program, "A Life Among Whales." Whales in one area were killed because fishermen believed the whales were threatening the fish supply. Then, the killer whales in the area, which had been feeding on the young whales, were forced to find other prey and killed seals. The number of seals declined dramatically, and the killer whales began eating otters. The decline in the number of otters led to an explosion in the populations of sea urchins and other animals the otters ate. The sea urchins and other animals destroyed the kelp forests, where young fish took shelter from predators. Predators ate the young fish, the fishery collapsed, and the fishermen could no longer earn a living. The fishermen's effort to protect their fishery wound up destroying it because they didn't recognize the interconnectedness of the ecosystem's biodiversity.

forests, and oceans also help biodiversity. Remember—everything is interconnected.

Prevent air, water, and soil pollution. Reduce your carbon footprint. Choose green products whenever you can. When you do have hazardous products, dispose of them properly to avoid creating pollution. Choose food and goods produced using sustainable, environmentally friendly methods. As much as possible, choose food and goods produced locally. Don't buy items that are made from endangered species or that threaten their habitats. Join a conservation organization. Write to government leaders. Let them know how

Trees add beauty and can help reduce the cost of cooling a home. Trees native to the area are best. They won't need lots of added water, fertilizer, or pesticide.

important it is to maintain biodiversity. Urge them to pass laws that will help fight global warming. Urge them to protect forests, oceans, and wilderness areas.

The challenges threatening biodiversity are enormous, and the need to act is great. The difficulties can seem overwhelming, but remember—even little steps make a difference. Plant a tree to shade a house and keep it cool, and you may keep up to 2,000 pounds (900 kg) of carbon out of the atmosphere, according to the Nature Conservancy. So, take that first step today, and encourage all your friends and family to take it with you. Working together, everyone can make wise choices about conservation and protect the planet!

TEN GREAT QUESTIONS TO ASK A SCIENCE TEACHER

 1. Which causes less pollution: using paper towels or electric hand dryers in public restrooms?

 2. When ocean water is desalinated to make drinking water for coastal communities, how does it affect the marine life in the area?

 3. How does climate change increase hurricane strength?

 4. Is burning coal to produce electricity less polluting than burning oil?

 5. Will melting glaciers change the oceans' salinity?

 6. Would using trains instead of trucks to transport goods reduce the amount of CO_2 put into the atmosphere?

 7. Why does underwater sonar cause marine mammals to beach themselves?

 8. Do forests speed up or slow down global warming?

 9. What is "global dimming" and what does it have to do with air pollution?

 10. Can offshore drilling and drilling in environmentally sensitive areas for oil and natural gas be done without causing environmental damage?

GLOSSARY

additives Substances added to something else, such as food, to affect a property, such as texture, color, or flavor.

aerator A device for mixing air into something.

bacteria Tiny living organisms that cannot be seen with the eye alone. Some bacteria cause illness or rotting, but others are helpful.

carbon footprint A measure of the impact human activities have on the environment in terms of the amount of greenhouse gases produced, measured in units of carbon dioxide.

chlorine A gas that is used in bleach and to purify water.

compost Decayed organic matter, such as leftover food, that is used as fertilizer.

corrode To wear away a little at a time.

dioxin A family of highly poisonous hydrocarbon compounds that are formed as a result of combustion processes, including burning trash and fuels like wood and coal.

emissions Substances put into the air by industry, automobiles, and various human activities.

endanger To put in danger or at risk.

erosion The wearing away of land over time.

extinction The state of no longer existing.

fisheries Places for catching fish or other marine animals.

invasive Describing an organism introduced into an area from outside and causing harm by spreading.

mileage The average number of miles a vehicle will travel on a gallon of gas that is used as a measure of fuel economy.

nutrients Food that a living organism needs to live and grow.

pesticides Poisons used to kill pests.

phosphates Compounds containing phosphorus that are used in fertilizers and some detergents.

photochemical smog Air pollution that results from a chemical reaction caused by sunlight.

photosynthesis The way in which green plants make their own food from sunlight, water, and a gas called carbon dioxide.

pollinate To spread pollen from one plant to another so that the plants can reproduce.

salvaged Recovered from rubbish as valuable or useful.

sediments Gravel, sand, or mud carried by wind or water.

sewage Waste.

sustainable Capable of being continued or maintained with little long-term effect on the environment.

thermostat A device for regulating indoor temperatures.

toxic Poisonous.

toxin A poisonous substance, especially one that is produced by a living organism.

watersheds Regions where water drains into a water supply, such as a river or lake.

weatherize To make something, such as a house, better protected against winter weather.

FOR MORE INFORMATION

Conservation International
2011 Crystal Drive, Suite 500
Arlington, VA 22202
(800) 429-5660 (in United States)
(703) 341-2400
Web site: http://www.conservation.org
Conservation International's mission is to conserve Earth's living
heritage—its global biodiversity—and demonstrate that human
societies are able to live harmoniously with nature.

Environment Canada
Inquiry Centre
70 Crémazie Street
Gatineau, QC K1A 0H3
Canada
(800) 668-6767 (in Canada)
(819) 997-2800
Web site: http://www.ec.gc.ca
Environment Canada's mission is to preserve and enhance the quality
of Canada's natural environment.

Evergreen
355 Adelaide Street West, Fifth Floor
Toronto, ON M5V 1S2
Canada
(416) 596-1495
Web site: http://www.evergreen.ca
Evergreen's goal is to benefit communities and nature by getting people
involved in maintaining a healthy, dynamic environment.

National Forest Protection Alliance
P.O. Box 8264
Missoula, MT 59807
(406) 542-7565
Web site: http://www.forestadvocate.org
The National Forest Protection Alliance is a network of organizations
that take action to protect and restore America's national forests.

Natural Resources Defense Council (NRDC)
40 West 20th Street
New York, NY 10011
(212) 727-2700
Web site: http://www.nrdc.org
Founded in 1970, the NRDC uses law and science to protect the
planet's wildlife and wild places and ensure a safe and healthy
environment for all living things.

The Nature Conservancy
4245 North Fairfax Drive, Suite 100
Arlington, VA 22203-1606
(703) 841-5300
Web site: http://www.nature.org
Founded in 1951, the Nature Conservancy works with local partners
around the world to protect ecologically important lands and
waters for nature and people.

U.S. Environmental Protection Agency
Ariel Rios Building
1200 Pennsylvania Avenue NW

Washington, DC 20460
(202) 272-0167
Web site: http://www.epa.gov
The U.S. Environmental Protection Agency was established in 1970 to
    protect people's health and the environment. The agency conducts
    research on environmental issues, develops and enforces regula-
    tions, and provides funding for research by universities and
    nonprofit organizations.

WEB SITES

Due to the changing nature of Internet links, Rosen Publishing has
developed an online list of Web sites related to the subject of this book.
This site is updated regularly. Please use this link to access the list:

http://www.rosenlinks.com/gre/cons

Adair, Rick. *Critical Perspectives on Politics and the Environment* (Scientific American Critical Anthologies on Environment and Climate). New York, NY: Rosen Publishing, 2006.

Calhoun, Yael, ed. *Conservation* (Environmental Issues). New York, NY: Chelsea House, 2005.

Daintith, John, and Jill Bailey, eds. *The Facts On File Dictionary of Ecology and the Environment*. New York, NY: Facts On File, 2003.

Dupler, Douglas. *Conserving the Environment* (Opposing Viewpoints). Farmington Hills, MI: Greenhaven Press, 2006.

Egendorf, Laura K. *The Environment* (Opposing Viewpoints). Farmington Hills, MI: Greenhaven Press, 2004.

Fridell, Ron. *Earth-Friendly Energy* (Saving Our Living Earth). Minneapolis, MN: Lerner Publications, 2009.

Gore, Al. *An Inconvenient Truth: The Planetary Emergency of Global Warming and What We Can Do About It*. New York, NY: Rodale, Inc., 2006.

Greenland, Paul R., and Annamarie L. Sheldon. *Career Opportunities in Conservation and the Environment*. New York, NY: Checkmark Books, 2007.

Orr, David W. *Earth in Mind: On Education, Environment, and the Human Prospect*. Rev. ed. Washington, DC: Island Press, 2004.

Wilcox, Charlotte. *Earth-Friendly Waste Management* (Saving Our Living Earth). Minneapolis, MN: Lerner Publications, 2009.

BIBLIOGRAPHY

Brooks, Oakley. "Standing Army: Fighting Climate Change by Protecting Forests." *Nature Conservancy*, Vol. 58, No. 2, Summer 2008, page 13.

Christensen, Anders, Roger Westerholm, and Jacob Almén. "Measurement of Regulated and Unregulated Exhaust Emissions from a Lawn Mower with and Without an Oxidizing Catalyst: A Comparison of Two Different Fuels." *Environmental Science & Technology*, Vol. 35, No. 11, June 1, 2001, pages 2,166–2,170.

Conservation International. "Saving Forests." Retrieved August 8, 2008 (http://www.conservation.org/learn/forests/Pages/overview.aspx).

Diaz, Robert J., and Rutger Rosenberg. "Spreading Dead Zones and Consequences for Marine Ecosystems." *Science*, Vol. 321, No. 5891, August 15, 2008, pages 926–929.

Downie, Andrew. "Growth Potential." *Nature Conservancy*, Vol. 58, No. 2, Summer 2008, pages 56–64.

Editors of *E/The Environmental Magazine*. *Green Living: The E Magazine Handbook for Living Lightly on the Earth*. New York, NY: Plume, 2005.

He, Congrong, Lidia Morawska, and Len Taplin. "Particle Emission Characteristics of Office Printers." *Environmental Science and Technology*, Vol. 14, No. 17, 2007, pages 6,039–6,045.

Invernizzi, Giovanni. "Particulate Matter from Tobacco Versus Diesel Car Exhaust: An Educational Perspective." *Tobacco Control*, Vol. 13, 2004, pages 219–221.

Millennium Ecosystem Assessment. *Ecosystems and Human Well-Being: Biodiversity Synthesis*. Washington, DC: World Resources Institute, 2005.

Natural Resources Defense Council. "Issues: Global Warming." Retrieved August 3, 2008 (http://www.nrdc.org/globalWarming/gsteps.asp).

Natural Resources Defense Council. "Issues: Health. Organic Foods 101." Retrieved August 3, 2008 (http://www.nrdc.org/health/farming/forg101.asp).

Natural Resources Defense Council. "Issues: Water." Retrieved September 7, 2008 (http://www.nrdc.org/water/default.asp).

Natural Resources Defense Council. "Issues: Wildlands." Retrieved September 22, 2008 (http://www.nrdc.org/landforests/fforestf.asp).

Nature Conservancy. "Climate Change: What You Can Do." Retrieved July 9, 2008 (http://www.nature.org/initiatives/climatechange/activities/art19631.html).

Nature Conservancy. "Have You Changed Your Climate Today?" *Nature Conservancy*, Vol. 57, No. 2, Summer 2007.

New York State Department of Environmental Conservation. "About Ozone." Retrieved August 3, 2008 (http://www.dec.ny.gov/public/337.html).

New York State Department of Environmental Conservation. "Green Living: 10 Things You Can Do to Help the Environment Right Now—Gas Saving Tips." Retrieved August 3, 2008 (http://www.dec.ny.gov/chemical/8400.html).

SAHRA (Sustainability of Semi-Arid Hydrology and Riparian Areas). "Gray Water Re-use." University of Arizona, 2001. Retrieved August 13, 2008 (http://www.sahra.arizona.edu/programs/water_cons/tips/re-use/gray.htm).

Shah, Anup. "Biodiversity." Global Issues, June 14, 2008. Retrieved August 11, 2008 (http://www.globalissues.org/EnvIssues/Biodiversity.asp).

Toropova, Caitlyn. "Everyday Environmentalist: Ask Where Your Food Comes From." *Nature Conservancy*. Retrieved July 8, 2008 (http://www.nature.org/activities/art23423.html).

INDEX

ABOUT THE AUTHOR

Janey Levy is a writer and editor who has written about one hundred books for children and young adult readers. She lives on three acres near Colden, New York, in an energy-efficient log house that uses a geothermal system to heat the house in the winter and cool it in the summer. She recycles, uses compact fluorescent bulbs and environmentally friendly household cleaners, and takes reusable bags to the grocery store. She chooses energy-efficient appliances and makes gas mileage a priority when buying a car. Levy is also a member of the Nature Conservancy.

PHOTO CREDITS

Cover, p. 1 © www.istockphoto.com/panorios; p. 7 © www.istockphoto.com/David Parsons; p. 9 Greenpeace/Reuters/Newscom; p. 12 © www.istockphoto.com/Kenneth C. Zirkel; p. 13 © www.istockphoto.com/Ryerson Clark; p. 14 © www.istockphoto.com/Corinne Lutter; p. 17 © www.istockphoto.com/Peter Finnie; p. 19 © David R. Frazier/The Image Works; p. 20 Mario Ruiz/Time & Life Pictures/Getty Images; p. 23 pasthinkstock/Newscom; p. 26 © www.istockphoto.com/Sebastien Cote; p. 27 © www.istockphoto.com/Pattie Calfy; p. 30 © Ron Sanford/Comet/Corbis; pp. 33, 34, 38, 41 © AP Images; p. 43 Yoshikazu Tsuno/AFP/Getty Images; p. 49 © Yuri Cortez/AFP/Getty Images; p. 52 © www.istockphoto.com/David Peeters.

Designer: Nicole Russo; Editor: Kathy Kuhtz Campbell;
Photo Researcher: Amy Feinberg